Adventurers

Program Authors

Connie Juel, Ph.D.

Jeanne R. Paratore, Ed.D.

Deborah Simmons, Ph.D.

Sharon Vaughn, Ph.D.

PEARSON

Scott
Foresman

Glenview, Illinois
Boston, Massachusetts
Chandler, Arizona
Upper Saddle River, New Jersey

ISBN-13: 978-0-328-45296-5
ISBN-10:   0-328-45296-3

9 10 11 12 13 V3NL 17 16 15 14 13
CC1

UNIT 5

Adventurers

Back in Time 5

How can we find adventure in historical events?

Finding Our Way 31

How does technology help us explore?

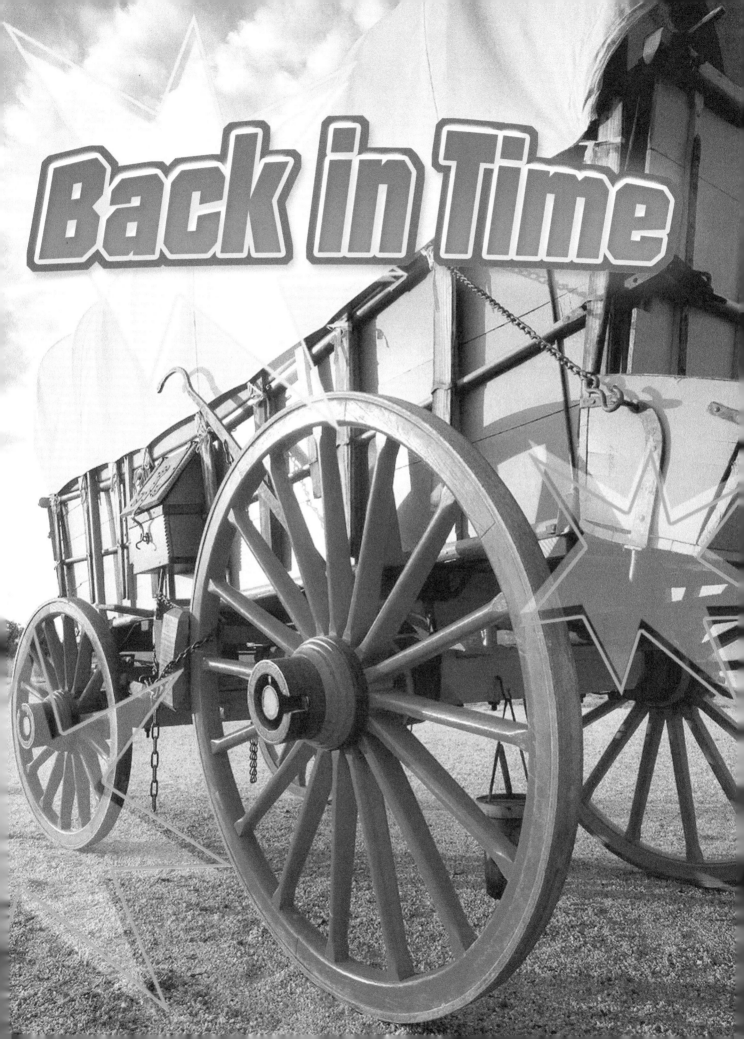

Back in Time

Contents

Back in Time

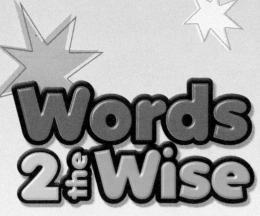

Words 2 the Wise

We can find adventure in our everyday lives. We can look **back in time** to find adventure too. As you read, think about adventures you can find in history.

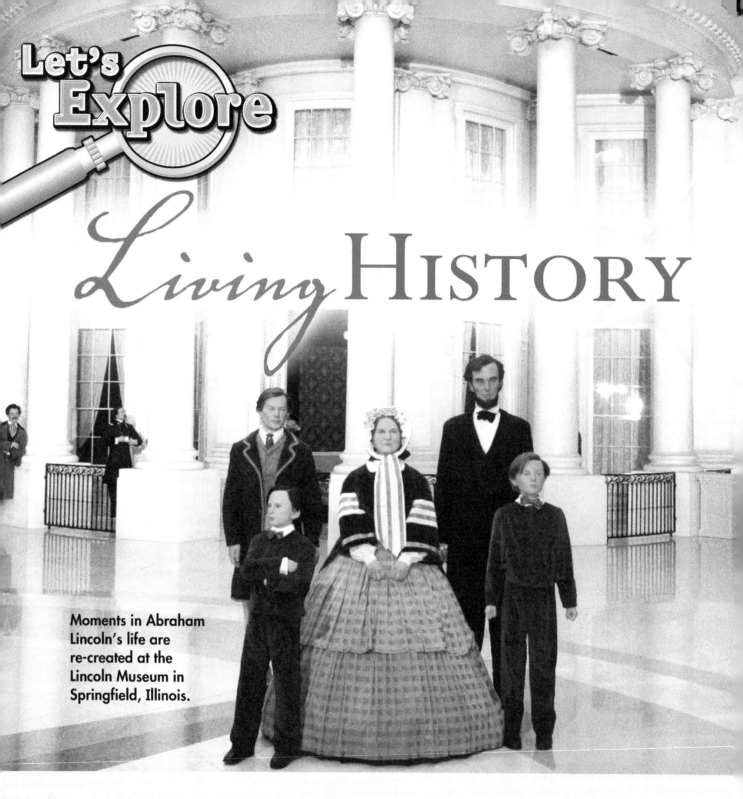

Let's Explore

Living HISTORY

Moments in Abraham Lincoln's life are re-created at the Lincoln Museum in Springfield, Illinois.

Wouldn't it be fun to step back in history and be there as historic moments happen? You can do just that at the Abraham Lincoln Library and Museum. This museum is in Springfield, Illinois. It's designed to make you feel like you are living through events that happened in history!

Rooms in the museum re-create important places and times in Lincoln's life. Visitors walk through his boyhood home, his first place of business, and the White House. They join the President on the last night of his life at Ford's Theater. Other rooms have objects from Lincoln's life. A library holds thousands of Lincoln's books and papers. These include papers Lincoln signed to outlaw slavery.

Other museums let visitors experience the past. Maybe one is near you!

This display shows Abraham Lincoln working with his cabinet.

The last moments of Lincoln's life are shown in Ford's Theater.

This display shows both sides of the debate to end slavery.

HANDS-On HISTORY

by Liese Vogel

You walk through the camp, which is buzzing with activity. You pass a group of soldiers. They are polishing guns called muskets. You stop to watch a woman make rope. The smell of baked bread floats through the air. In the distance you hear beating drums.

Someone nearby speaks loudly in French. He is selling animal skins. You run your hands over a pile of furs. They feel soft and silky.

This is how trading looked long ago.

Fort de Chartres sits along the Mississippi River in southern Illinois.

As you walk on, you pass beneath stone arches and into the great fort.

Are you a young person who lived long ago? No! You're in the present-day, and you're visiting an 18th century French fort in southern Illinois. It's called Fort de Chartres (shart). The French built this fort in the 1750s. Each year thousands of visitors come here for the annual rendezvous (RON-day-voo).

Rendezvous is a French word. It means "meeting planned at a certain time and place." This historical rendezvous is a reenactment of one that used to happen in this area each year in the 1700s. Fur trappers and traders would buy and sell animal skins. Other people came to sell goods too.

France lost this land to Great Britain in 1763. The people stopped using Fort de Chartres. In 1913 the State of Illinois bought the site and rebuilt the fort.

Inside the walls of the fort, visitors experience sights and sounds from the 1750s.

Today, the rendezvous takes place here each June. Thousands of volunteers come from around the country to re-create eighteenth-century life. The public enjoys seeing history come alive. The volunteers dress as fur trappers, traders, settlers, and soldiers. They set up shelters for sleeping.

Volunteers act as their characters did long ago. They display furs, pottery, baskets, quilts, or other goods. They make arrows, horseshoes, rope, or barrels.

Volunteers master crafts that are no longer common, such as making horseshoes.

Visitors spend the weekend walking throughout the camp. They can watch people shoot bows and fire guns. They can talk with the actors and even buy some of their goods. People sell food, candles, children's toys, and blankets. Entertainment includes live music and theater. Visitors can also tour the fort to learn its history and the history of the fur trade.

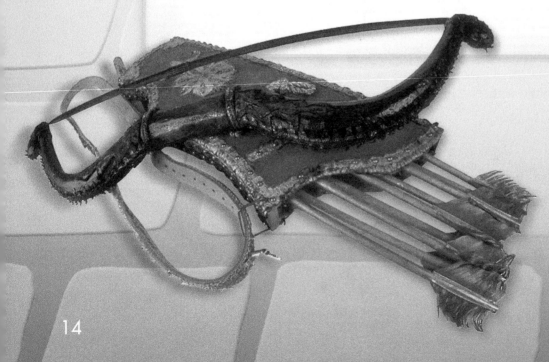

The reenactment can astonish viewers. Smoke and gunshots fill the air. Actors practice military drills. Cannons are fired. The sights and sounds of the 1700s come alive.

Actors work hard to re-create true history. They like to answer people's questions about their characters and historical events. They spend hours studying how their characters lived and worked.

Cannons are fired as part of the reenactments.

When actors are performing, they must look and sound real. They learn their characters' languages and carefully choose costumes and props. They learn to use tools that might not be used today. Actors must also act in a safe, professional way at all times.

For people in the fur trade, going to a rendezvous was the highlight of their year. They were able to share goods and information.

Actors live like their characters did in the 1700s.

Fur trappers and traders held rendezvous throughout the wilderness in the 1700s and 1800s. These events are reenacted today in many modern cities and towns.

The rendezvous at Fort de Chartres is one of the oldest and the biggest. Let the reenactments at the annual rendezvous astonish you!

These volunteers prepare for a battle reenactment.

What Do You Think?

Why do people enjoy participating in the annual rendezvous at Fort de Chartres?

Kristen's Dance

by Catherine M. Ives

illustrated by Maurie J. Manning

The trip to the Northwest Historic Museum was just about to end. Kristen, Noah, Sara, and Pete were walking through the last exhibit very slowly. Brightly colored beads sparkled on Native American outfits. Eagle feathers were attached to buckskin. Moccasins were in display cases.

"Why are the clothes so fancy?" Noah asked the museum guide.

"These clothes were worn for celebrations," he replied.

"Do people still know how to make this kind of outfit?" asked Pete.

"Parents remember the tradition and teach their children to make traditional outfits with buckskin, beads, ribbons, and jingles," said the guide.

"What are those?" asked Kristen curiously.

"Jingles. When women dance, the jingles ring with every step," he answered.

Kristen thought of her ballet costume. Her tutu had a silky top with sequins and a ruffled skirt. But, it didn't make music when she moved!

"Can we watch this kind of dancing?" Kristen asked the guide.

"Competitions are starting in the powwow tents. You can watch dances that are a part of Native American culture."

Ms. Santos and the class headed for the powwow tents.

Now Kristen was even more curious to see the dance performance. She was a dancer. Could she watch and pick up the movements and steps? But she had no jingle dress to join in the dance. They all went inside the tent.

DANCE
COMPETITION

Grass Dance 1 PM
Ribbon Dance 1:30
Jingle Dance 2 PM

"Watch the dancers in the circle," Ms. Santos said. "Remember, we are guests. Watch respectfully," she explained.

"There she is!" clapped the lady next to Kristen.

"This is my granddaughter's first powwow competition," she said proudly. "I'm Mrs. Chapoose."

"I'm Kristen. Did you help her make her dress?" she asked.

"Yes, we sewed jingles on until that dress could sing," she laughed.

21

"I'm a dancer too," said Kristen. "But my outfit doesn't sing. In ballet class we dance to music that tells a story, like *Sleeping Beauty.* I'll be performing in a ballet soon. Does the jingle dancing tell a story?"

"There is a story about the jingle dress. Each time dancers wear the dress, they re-create that story and honor the tradition," replied Mrs. Chapoose. "This is the story I learned."

"The Ojibway (oh-JIB-way) Nation lived near the Great Lakes. A man had a daughter who was very sick. One night, he had a dream. The man saw women dancing in jingle dresses. When he awoke, he told his wife the dream. Together, they made a jingle dress for their daughter. The people came and sang to her. The daughter got up and danced in the dress. She was well!"

"So jingle dancing and ballet tell a story," said Kristen.

I like jingle dancing, Kristen thought as she watched.

During a break Mrs. Chapoose said, "You were watching those dancers' steps. Show me what you can do."

Kristen remembered the sound of the drum beat. Left-hop-hop. Right-hop-hop. She placed her hands on her hips like the dancers.

"Imagine you have an eagle feather in your hair and a beaded purse at your waist," said Mrs. Chapoose. "Remember the sound of the jingles." She smiled.

That night, Kristen looked at her ballet outfit. She felt that it was missing something. It didn't have jingles like Mrs. Chapoose's granddaughter's outfit. But then she remembered something important. She still had a story to tell—just like the jingle dancers.

At the performance, her class took the stage and the piano music started. With a twirl and a leap, Kristen began to dance. Her heart swelled with pride as she told the story of *Sleeping Beauty*.

What Do You Think?

Did Kristen enjoy the powwow?
How do you know?

A Song's Secret Code

"Follow the Drinking Gourd" is a song that told slaves how to escape to the North during the Civil War. The Drinking Gourd was a secret code for the Big Dipper. The Big Dipper is a group of stars that looks like a dipper.

Follow the Drinking Gourd

Stanza 1

When the sun comes back and the first quail calls,
Follow the drinking gourd.
For the old man is waiting for to carry you to freedom
If you follow the drinking gourd.

The beginning tells slaves to travel during winter. Frozen rivers are easier to cross. "Follow the drinking gourd" means keep the Big Dipper in sight. The old man was Peg Leg Joe. He had a wooden leg. He would help them escape.

Chorus

Follow the drinking gourd!
Follow the drinking gourd!
For the old man is waiting for to carry you to freedom
If you follow the drinking gourd.

Stanza 2

The riverbank makes a very good road,
The dead trees will show you the way,
Left foot, peg foot traveling on,
Following the drinking gourd.

The second stanza tells the slaves to follow the river and go north. Peg Leg Joe's tracks are along the river bank. His tracks are a pattern of footprint-wooden peg, footprint-wooden peg.

The Big Dipper is a pattern of stars that looks like a long-handled dipper for drinking water. A gourd was also used as a dipper for drinking water.

In this painting, runaway slaves find safe shelter.

Stanza 3

The river ends between two hills,
Follow the drinking gourd.
There's another river on the other side,
Follow the drinking gourd.

This stanza tells the slaves to follow the river to where it begins. Slaves should cross over the hills to the Tennessee River and keep heading north. The song told about natural landmarks like rivers and stars. The slaves had no maps.

(Repeat *Chorus*)

Stanza 4

Where the great big river meets the little river,
Follow the drinking gourd.
The old man is waiting for to carry you to freedom
If you follow the drinking gourd.

The last stanza tells slaves to follow the rivers north. The small Tennessee River meets the bigger Ohio River. Slaves had to find a guide from the Underground Railroad to help them cross the Ohio River. They would then follow the Big Dipper to escape to the North.

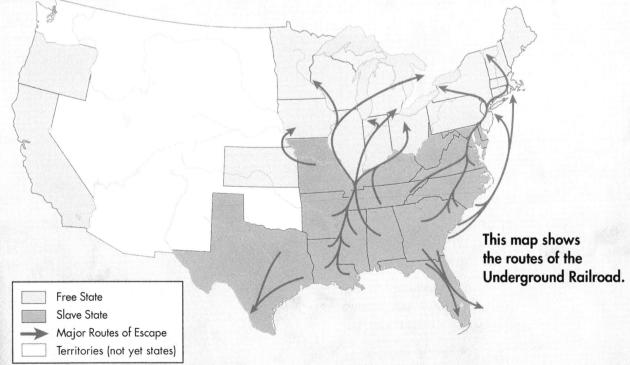

This map shows the routes of the Underground Railroad.

- Free State
- Slave State
- → Major Routes of Escape
- Territories (not yet states)

4 You 2 Do

Word Play

Did you know the word *astonish* comes from a Latin word meaning "thunder"? People who are astonished sometimes say they are "thunderstruck." Think of words that mean the same as *astonish*. Use the dictionary for help.

Making Connections

How do reenactments and museums help people feel like they are a part of history?

On Paper

Imagine that you could go back in time to the 1800s. What question would you ask someone from that time? Why?

Possible answers to Word Play:
amaze, overwhelm, surprise,
shock, dumbfound, astound

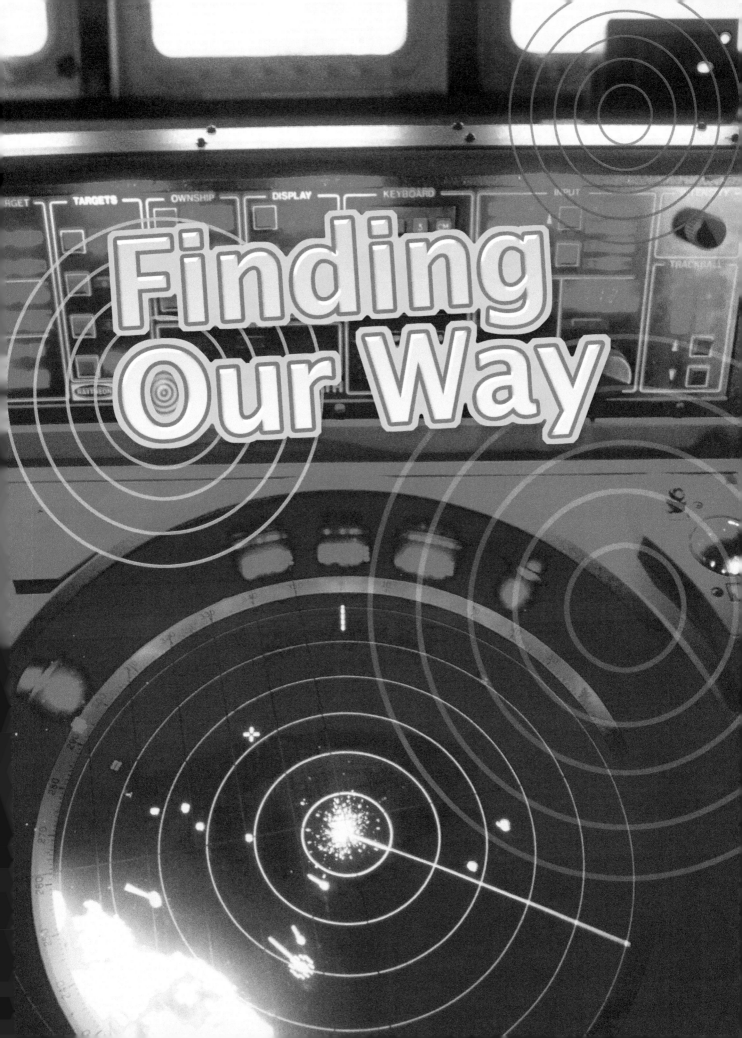

Contents

Finding Our Way

Let's Explore

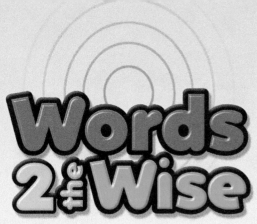
Words 2 the Wise

Technology helps us find our way around the world. As you read, think about how **technology and adventures** can help us reach new places.

Let's Explore WHERE WE ARE

A sextant, compass, and charts helped explorers cross oceans and reach unmapped lands.

Sailors once found their way with a compass, sextant, and sea charts. Now all kinds of technology can tell us where we are and help us get where we are going.

Ships can cross the sea using Global Positioning System (GPS). GPS uses signals from satellites to locate any spot on Earth. Cars, cell phones, and even watches are equipped with GPS.

Technology helps scientists track the migration habits of whales.

Sonar stands for **so**und **n**avigation **a**nd **r**anging. It uses sound waves to find objects underwater. Sonar helps locate sunken treasure and sea life. It has even been used to search for the Loch Ness Monster!

Air traffic controllers use radar to safely guide airplanes. Radar stands for **ra**dio **d**etection **a**nd **r**anging. On a radar screen, airplanes look like tiny blips of light.

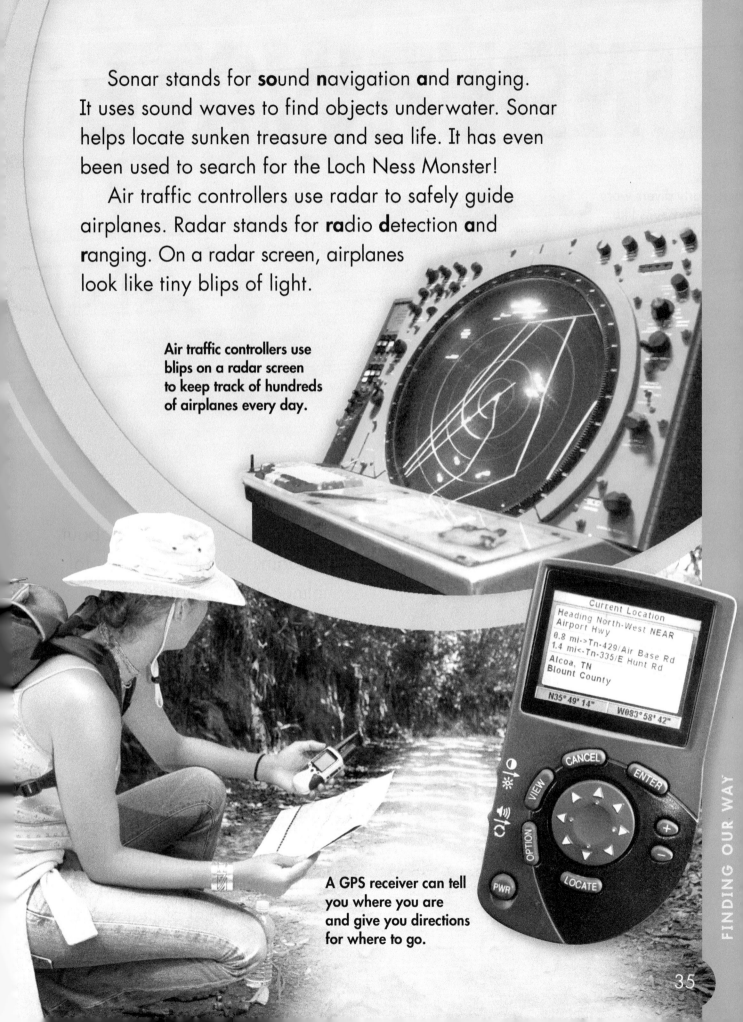

Air traffic controllers use blips on a radar screen to keep track of hundreds of airplanes every day.

Current Location
Heading North-West NEAR
Airport Hwy
0.8 mi->Tn-429/Air Base Rd
1.4 mi<-Tn-335/E Hunt Rd
Alcoa, TN
Blount County
N35° 49' 14"   W083° 58' 42"

CANCEL   ENTER
VIEW
OPTION
PWR   LOCATE

A GPS receiver can tell you where you are and give you directions for where to go.

UNDERWATER HIDE AND SEEK

BY PATRICIA MCFADDEN

Early divers wore heavy suits like this one.

1906

Your big adventure is about to begin. You attach the metal helmet to your leather diving suit. You make sure the air hose is working. Splash! You hit the water and sink like a rock.

You reach the sea floor and shine your light around. You know that somewhere nearby there is a sunken ship.

How you wish there were a way to locate it in the middle of the sea!

There! A glint of metal. You found it!

Diving gear today is not as bulky as it was 100 years ago.

Today

It's time to go to work. You zip up your wet suit and pull on your goggles. Then you strap on an air tank and jump into the water. You are part of an expedition that is mapping the ancient part of Alexandria, Egypt that sank underwater. You swim through the murky water until you find what you are looking for.

It's the large vase that has been hidden beneath the waves for seven hundred years.

Far above you, a Global Positioning System (GPS) receiver is bobbing on the waves. Your job is to connect a line from it to the vase. The next time someone wants to find the vase, GPS will locate it. Other divers will be able to go right to the same place. This allows more time for new exploration.

Also a new kind of adventure may be possible with GPS. Some historians want to turn Alexandria into an underwater museum. Divers would rent scuba gear and swim down to see the ruins. A map created with GPS technology could show divers where to find every vase.

Underwater expeditions and treasure hunts are costly. GPS saves time and money.

This diver could attach a GPS receiver to the vase so that others can find it later.

Alexandria

Alexandria was one of the great cities of Egypt. It had palaces and great libraries. A huge lighthouse stood in Alexandria's harbor.

In the 1300s the lighthouse and much of Alexandria were destroyed by an earthquake and sank into the sea.

Alexandria's lighthouse was one of the Seven Wonders of the Ancient World.

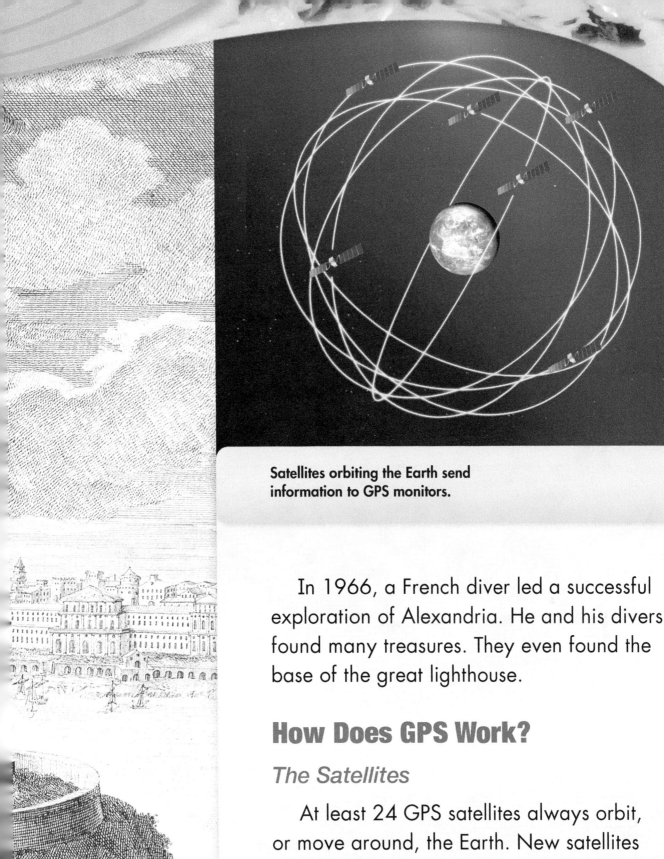

Satellites orbiting the Earth send information to GPS monitors.

In 1966, a French diver led a successful exploration of Alexandria. He and his divers found many treasures. They even found the base of the great lighthouse.

How Does GPS Work?

The Satellites

At least 24 GPS satellites always orbit, or move around, the Earth. New satellites are launched into space when the old ones wear out.

It takes the satellites 12 hours to make a complete orbit.

The Tracking Stations

Tracking stations are all over the world. They monitor the satellites. The master control station is in Colorado. It monitors the other tracking stations. If a satellite breaks down, a tracking station reports it. A new satellite will be sent into orbit.

Receivers

A GPS receiver picks up signals from the satellites. It must get signals from at least four satellites. A GPS receiver can tell you exactly where you are.

Tracking stations receive information from satellites.

Uses

GPS is used in many ways. Children carry GPS receivers so their parents can find them. Wild animals and even some pets have GPS receivers. Ships, airplanes, and cars use GPS. GPS is in some cell phones too. Where would you go with GPS technology?

WHAT DO YOU THINK?

How has GPS changed the way we locate things?

Scale: 450 yd

318ft

GPS receivers in cars use information from satellites to tell you where you are.

RESCUED!

by John Manos

illustrated by
Ruth Palmer

Mark was scared. As an experienced pilot, he knew when his small plane didn't feel right in the sky. He was high above the Rocky Mountains in Montana, and there was no place to land.

The air traffic controller heard the message that Mark was in trouble. Then the plane disappeared from the controller's radar screen. Mark was lost somewhere in the mountains, and night was falling!

Callie Roundtree's Search and Rescue (SAR) team was doing a drill that night. Callie got a call that a pilot was lost nearby. Callie was glad he wouldn't have to wait hours to be rescued. With the proper equipment, her team would find him in no time!

But will we discover him before it's too late? Callie wondered. It's night, and we don't know where he is!

As team leader, Callie had to organize the rescue. She called everyone together.

"A rescue plane will send out a signal. The signal will find the lost pilot's GPS* receiver," she said. "The rescue plane will tell us the wrecked plane's location."

She looked at the team members. "This isn't a drill," she said. "This is a real mission. There's someone lost in the mountains who needs our help. Are you ready?"

Everyone cheered.

*GPS Global Positioning System

The rescue pilot saw a burning wreck before he got a GPS signal. It looked like the lost pilot didn't have a chance.

But then the rescue pilot radioed Callie and her team. "I'm getting a weak signal about a mile from the burning plane! The pilot must have a cell phone with a GPS chip."

Instantly, the SAR team was on its way in the direction of the lost pilot.

Callie had to remind herself that the night's adventure was real, because it seemed just like the tracking drills her SAR team had practiced before.

She spread out the maps of the area. She used a compass to mark the direction of the lost pilot.

Groups of four searchers spread out over a half-mile area and worked their way uphill, but it was slow going. They had to locate Mark as soon as possible.

Each group called to one another while they searched. They carried radios and other equipment.

But they were worried. Their maps showed them where they were, but the maps were hard to follow. It was hard to picture what the land was like from a map. Mark might be in any small hollow, and they could walk right past him!

Callie remembered that she had read about a computer program that made three-dimensional maps of the land. With one of these maps and the GPS location from the cell phone, they could find Mark quickly! Callie went to the map Web site on her laptop computer.

She blew her whistle in three short bursts. Everyone in the SAR groups knew that meant to stand still.

"Everyone wait!" she called into her radio.
"We're going to save this pilot!" She found
a three-dimensional map of the area on the
Internet. Then she used her walkie-talkie to
direct one SAR group to Mark's location.

The group members yelled Mark's name as
they climbed into the darkness. José, who had
night-vision goggles, was the first to spot the
injured pilot.

Mark's arm was broken. But thanks to Callie
and the SAR team, Mark had survived!

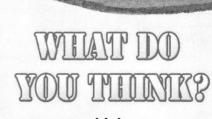

WHAT DO YOU THINK?

How would the rescue
have been different without
technology to help?

Behind the Screen

The Start of Video Game Entertainment

Video games have been around since the late 1950s. But games from the past look very different from today's video games. People around the world spend lots of time trying to beat their best scores. What does it take to design a video game?

Robert Thompson can tell you. It's his job!

Q: Robert, what is your title?

A: I'm a software engineer programmer. I help design video games.

Video games became
very popular in the 1980s.

Video games have become more advanced in the twenty-first century.

Q: What were you like as a child?

A: I really liked competition. I liked sports. But I really enjoyed video games. I liked being in a fantasy world. You get to do things that you just can't do in real life.

Q: What skills do you need for your job?

A: I have a math degree. I use math every day in my job. Math is very important in 3-D video games.

Q: What makes a good video game?

A: I judge a game by the way it feels. If the characters move in a way that seems real, that's a good sign.

Q: How has technology changed in the past ten years?

A: The 3-D images have really developed. If you look at video games from a decade ago, they look fake. Now special effects, like lightning and waterfalls, are awesome.

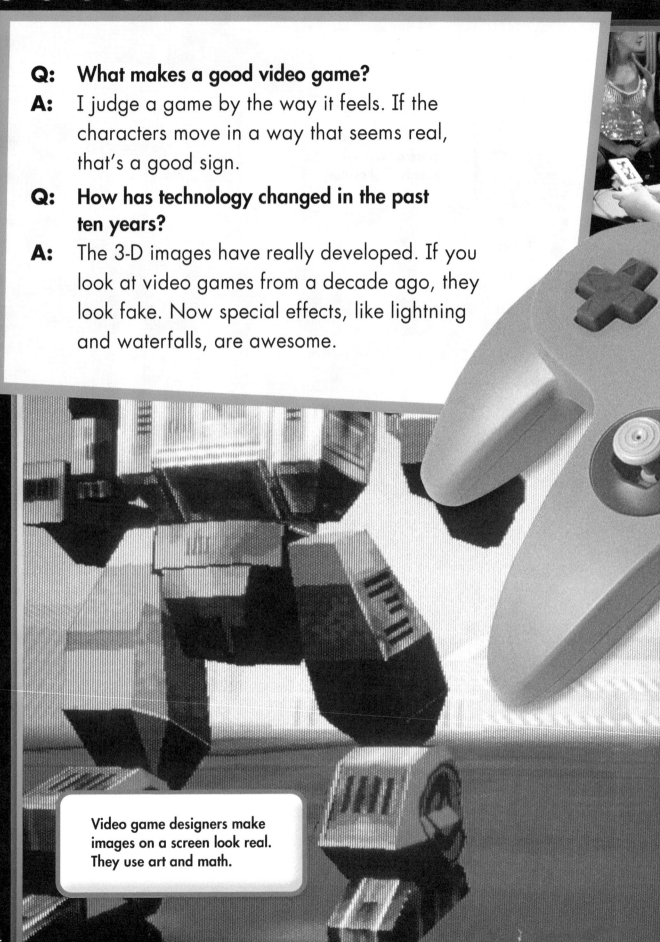

Video game designers make images on a screen look real. They use art and math.

New video games allow players around the world to compete with each other.

Q: What's your favorite video game?

A: I like *Mario Kart*. It's pretty simple and easy to learn. But this game becomes very competitive. It can keep a player on the edge of his or her seat. You need good hand-eye coordination.

Q: What else is different about video games now?

A: They allow you to play with other players. You can play with players in the same room, or you can play over the Internet. The players could be across the country.

4 you 2 Do

Word Play

How many smaller words can you find in the word EXPLORATION

Making Connections

How is technology used to explore on land and under the sea similar? How is it different?

On Paper

What new methods of exploration did you learn about? Which were the most interesting?

Possible answers to Word Play:
pin, tin, tear, rat, rate, pat, pale,
plate, explain, ration, rope.

Somewhere Out There

Contents

Somewhere Out There

Let's Explore

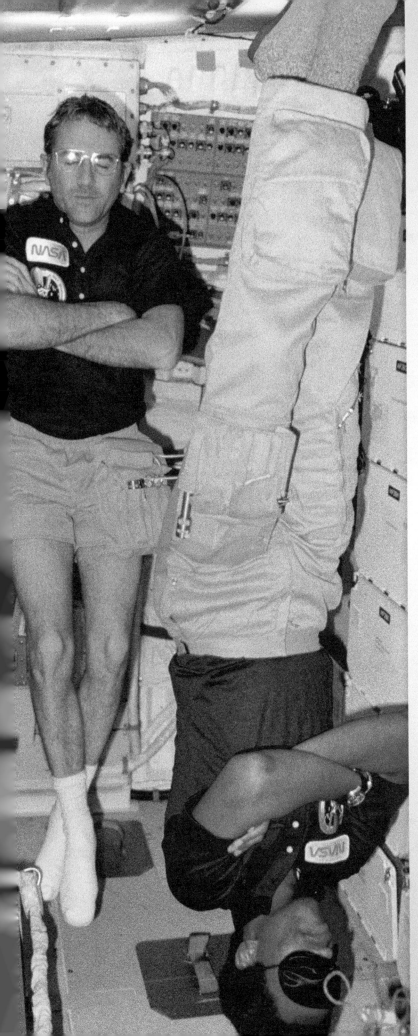

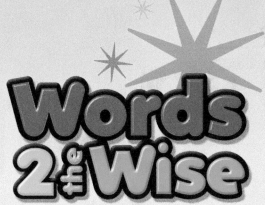

Words 2 the Wise

Astronauts have many **adventures in space.** Many of their discoveries have changed our lives on Earth. As you read, think about some of the things you might have because of space travel.

Let's Explore

Outer Space

Saturn

Venus

Mars

Mercury

Earth

Jupiter

Uranus

Neptune

Space exploration can go beyond the planets of our solar system.

When you hear the weather report, do you think about where the information comes from? Scientists send satellites into space. The satellites orbit the Earth and send back reports. People use this information every day in business and science. Some use it to save lives!

Humans have always wondered about the unknown. For many years people imagined what the moon was like. They wanted to know about the galaxies* beyond Earth. Telescopes could not answer all of people's questions. So space exploration began. A trip to the moon became a reality.

*galaxies very large groups of stars. Our galaxy is the Milky Way.

Astronauts need to check satellites and make repairs.

Now we explore far beyond the moon. Scientists launched the Mars *Odyssey* in 2001. It orbits Mars and sends photographs back to Earth. It also carries science experiments. Does Mars have water? Does life exist on Mars? People on Earth are trying to learn the answers to these questions.

The Mars *Odyssey* collected information about Mars for 917 days. This is a full year on Mars.

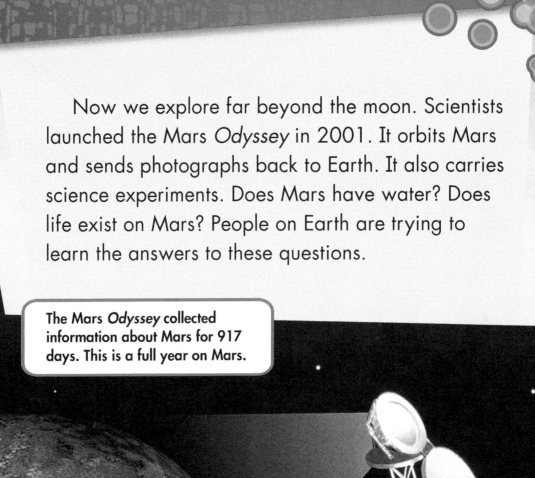

On Earth, astronauts in training fly T-38 jets.

We have accomplished much in space exploration. A man first walked on the moon in 1969. The shuttle *Discovery* launched the Hubble Space Telescope into orbit in 1990. Scientists have also launched space probes to study the sun, Jupiter, and Venus. People now live at the *International Space Station*.

Exploration answers questions. Exploration leads to new questions. Where is the next unknown? Where will explorations of the future go?

Life in Space

by Lorraine McCombs

NASA discovered how to make everyday tasks easy for space travel.

Men and women travel to outer space and explore new territory. It's completely different there. But they must do some of the same tasks that we do on Earth. Eating, sleeping, and washing are parts of our daily lives. But in space it's harder to do these than you might think.

Scientists taste the foods
to make them better.

Rehydratable
Food

Space Food

How do astronauts eat? They don't have stoves,
refrigerators, or stores.

The teams at NASA* plan the meals months in
advance. The foods must be nutritious. They must fit
into the small space on a space shuttle. NASA prepares
foods like eggs or even shrimp cocktail in powdered
form. The food is then sealed in plastic containers.

The space shuttle carries just enough food for each
day. Two extra meals per person are saved for
an emergency.

*NASA National Aeronautics and Space Administration

Food is fastened in place so that it does not float.

Imagine that you are inside the space shuttle. If you let go of a pencil, it floats around in the air. Now imagine eating a meal there.

How do the astronauts do this simple task? They strap a meal tray to their laps. The tray keeps the different containers from floating away.

Each astronaut receives a hygiene kit. The kit has things like toothbrushes and combs in it.

Imagine adding salt and pepper to your food while in space. Salt grains would float around the air! NASA provides salt that is dissolved in water and pepper mixed with oil to solve this problem.

Space Hygiene*

Astronauts can't step into a shower or fill a bathtub with water. NASA uses shampoo that astronauts don't have to rinse out of their hair. But they do use tiny amounts of water for brushing teeth.

*Hygiene how to stay clean and healthy

Astronauts wear ordinary clothes. They put on spacesuits only for launch, reentry, and work outside the shuttle.

Have you ever used the restroom on an airplane? The space shuttle restroom is similar except that astronauts strap their legs into place. The toilet works like a vacuum!

Space Laundry

Where do missing socks turn up at your house? On a space shuttle, they might be stuck to air vents! Astronauts who live on the *International Space Station* can't bring a lot of clothes. And they can't do laundry. Astronauts need to make their clothes last.

At the *International Space Station,* astronauts change their work shirts and pants every ten days and socks every other day. Astronauts have to keep fit in space. When they exercise, they wear the same T-shirts for three days.

Shuttle astronauts bring their worn clothes back to Earth. Space station astronauts put their clothes in a container that burns up when returning to Earth!

Astronauts wear white suits because the color reflects heat. The astronauts will stay cool inside the suit. Also astronauts are easier to see in white.

Astronaut Richard M. Linnehan
squeezes into the sleeping area
of the space shuttle *Columbia*.

Space Sleep

Outer space is big, but the space inside the shuttle is small. The crew has to live together in a small area. They must share a small sleeping space with their companions.

What did NASA plan for sleeping? Straps! With no gravity, astronauts have to be strapped down when they sleep. Sunlight can wake the sleeping crew.

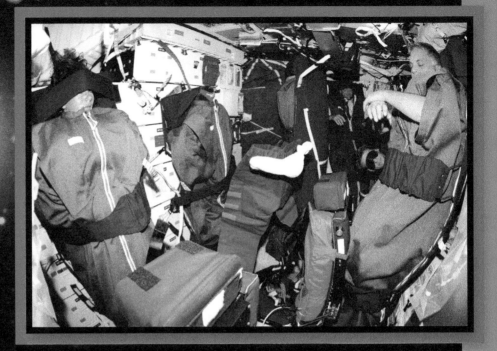

Astronauts can get comfortable in space, but they probably look forward to showers, beds, and clean laundry on Earth.

When it is time for the crew to wake up, Mission Control in Houston, Texas, plays wake-up music. The song might be a favorite of one of the astronauts. An astronaut's family might ask for a favorite song. Mission Control plays it, just like a radio D.J.

With or without music, life in outer space is a challenge. But astronauts are up to the challenge! Ready. Set. Blast off!

What Do You Think?

What challenges do astronauts face? How do they overcome them?

Thanks TO SPACE

by Marcus Wheeler

Did you know that many of the products that you use in your daily life were invented because of space exploration?

Scientists at NASA* need new products to explore space. They work with companies to invent the new products. Astronauts use the products on space missions. If those products work, the companies figure out how consumers like you can use them.

*__NASA__ National Aeronautics and Space Administration

Astronauts used bar codes to track what items were on the spacecraft. Now store clerks scan bar codes on items in grocery stores.

Golf Balls That Go the Distance

The space program needed to examine how engines run. So NASA invented video cameras that could film very fast. Golf companies used this video equipment to examine golf balls traveling through the air. They used this information to arrange the dents, or dimples, in a triangle pattern. The balls went farther!

Thanks to NASA, golf balls now travel faster than before.

Faster Wheels

Have you ever seen a bicycle wheel with wide spokes? Those spokes are a design that came from the space program. NASA had to design wings that forced objects to travel faster. One design had three wings. Now some bicycle wheels have three spokes. The spokes work like wings. The bicycles go faster with the new design.

A bicycle wheel usually has 32 or 36 spokes. This one has three.

Speedy Swimsuits

What slows down a shuttle when it travels? Air! Scientists made tiny grooves, or riblets, on the surface of the shuttle. The riblets made the shuttle travel faster. Could riblets help swimmers travel faster through water? Swimsuit makers thought so. Now some swimsuits have tiny riblets too. Swimmers who wear these suits move faster through the water!

A swimmer's chest has to push hard against water, so this swimsuit has riblets on the chest.

Ceramic Braces

Spacecraft and aircraft fly through extreme heat and cold. The parts must stand up to great pressure. Metals are strong. But NASA needed a new material. It made a type of clear ceramic that was tough. Now braces for teeth are made with this new ceramic material. These braces aren't as easy to see as metal braces.

Metal braces might become a thing of the past thanks to ceramic braces.

Sun-blocker Glasses

The sun's rays can hurt your eyes on Earth. Astronauts get even closer to the sun. So NASA had to figure out a way to protect astronauts' eyes. This time the solution was a new type of window. This window blocked the sun's rays while it let in the view. It wasn't long before stores were selling cool sunglasses made with the same type of sun-blocking material.

Space exploration also helped develop the lenses that don't scratch and ski goggles that don't fog up.

Cordless Tools

Astronauts needed tools to collect samples from the moon, but power tools all had cords. Astronauts couldn't plug a cord into an outlet. So scientists invented tools that were cordless. In time, consumers were able to buy the same type of electric appliances. They were using cordless telephones, drills, and vacuum cleaners because of the space program.

NASA astronauts use cordless power tools to work in space. We use them on Earth too.

NASA's technology led to many inventions. The work done by NASA scientists and astronauts can be found in stores, homes, and hospitals around the world.

With the next space mission, what new clothes, devices, or games will land in your home?

All these products were inspired by NASA and the space program.

What Do You Think?

How has space exploration helped us?

How Strange It Is

by Claudia Lewis

In the sky
Soft clouds are blowing by.
Nothing more can I see
In the blue air over me.

Yet I know that planetoids and rocket cones,
Telstars studded with blue stones,
And many hundred bits of fins
And other man-made odds and ends
Are wheeling round me out in space
At a breathless astronautic pace.

How strange it is to know
That while I watch the soft clouds blow
So many things I cannot see
Are passing by right over me.

Night Sky

by Zaro Weil

Night sky
Floods my room
Oh
My heart pounds
The moon is
Now my own.

4 You 2 Do

Word Play

Match these words with the word
or phrase that best describes them.

1. shuttle   a. group of workers
2. crew   b. buyer
3. companion   c. spaceship
4. consumer   d. partner

Making Connections

What things do you use that
came from space exploration?
Why are they important to you?

On Paper

Astronauts find new ways
to complete everyday tasks
aboard the space shuttle.
What part of eating,
sleeping, or dressing at home
would be more exciting to
do in space? Why?

Answers to Word Play:
1, c; 2, a; 3, d; 4, b.

Can You Dig It?

Contents

Can You Dig It?

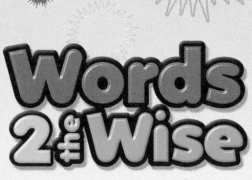

Words 2 the Wise

While we walk, run, and jump, a lot is happening beneath our feet. Underground explorers teach us what happens there. As you read, think about what explorers might encounter on their **adventures underground.**

UNDER

A lot goes on beneath our feet! Some of those things are natural. Others are things that humans have made. Let's look at what can happen under the ground below us.

There are miles of pipes under every city that deliver water to homes and buildings. They also carry waste from our sinks and toilets from our houses.

Caves have stalagmites and stalactites. These are like rock icicles. Stalagmites rise from the ground. Stalactites hang from the ceiling of a cave.

GROUND

The subway in London, England, is called the Tube. Can you guess why?

We have created places underground to travel and shop.

87

In a Cave

by George Reddick

What Is a Cave?

A cave is an opening in the ground. Caves can be large or small. A large cave, called a cavern, may be as large as a football field. Caves may have pathways that go on for miles.

Caves can be found all over the world. Every state in the United States has caves.

Stalactites hang from the ceiling.
Stalagmites grow up from the ground.

Try this to remember the difference between stalactites and stalagmites.

Stalac**tites** hang **tight.**

Stalag**mites might** grow up to the ceiling.

Stalac**tites**

Stalag**mites**

Caves can be explored for fun. A traveler or tourist can take a guided tour of a cave in many national parks of the United States.

On a cave tour you can see stalactites hanging from the top of the cave. Stalactites look like ice cream cones hanging from the cave's ceiling. They form from dripping water.

You can also see stalagmites. Stalagmites grow up from the cave floor.

Four teenagers discovered the Lascaux Cave in 1940. The cave was closed to the public in 1963 to preserve the paintings.

Old Uses

People who study caves know that prehistoric people used caves for homes. Lascaux (las-COH) Cave, a famous cave in France, has drawings that were made by humans over 17,000 years ago!

If prehistoric people used caves, why can't modern-day people use caves? They can! A cave in Bowling Green, Kentucky, was once a nightclub. Now it's a popular place for weddings and banquets.

Disguised burial caves have been discovered in countries all around the world.

Caves have also been used as burial sites. A family would have its own burial cave in ancient times. Sometimes they buried valuables with the body. Families kept the locations of these caves secret so that no one could disturb the dead or steal the objects.

Some families built stone walls to hide the entrance to the cave. The walls blended into the surrounding cliffs.

Cave-In-Rock was a dangerous place to pass on the Ohio River.

Caves and Outlaws

Caves were also hiding places. Pirates used Cave-In-Rock during the late 1790s. This cave was near the Ohio River in Hardin County, Illinois. Pirates would hide and wait for riverboats. When boats came by, they would rob the people on the boat and then hide in the cave.

$5,000.00

REWARD

Wanted by the State of Missouri

JESSE & FRANK JAMES

For Train Robbery

Notify AUTHORITIES
LIBERTY, MISSOURI

Signs like these offered rewards
for the capture of outlaws.

In the 1800s criminals used Cave-In-Rock to make fake money. By 1830 many settlers began to pass the cave on their way west. This made it easier for the robbers and outlaws to be caught. They stopped using the cave. The settlers took over the cave and used it as a resting place on their way west.

Many Jewish families escaped to the Priest's Grotto.

Caves as Safe Havens

During World War II, Jewish families were in great danger. The German Army arrested Jewish people. In 1942 a group of families packed their belongings and headed for a secret cavern in Ukraine called the Priest's Grotto.

The group had stayed in the cavern for 344 days. A friend lowered a bottle with a message through a hole in the ground when it was safe to leave. No other humans had ever lived that long underground. The cave protected them from the German Army.

Caves have had many uses over the years. Who knows how they will be used in the future?

What Do You Think?

How have caves been used differently over time?

BENEATH Our Feet

by Carol Pugliano-Martin
illustrated by Lynda Cohen

"Hey, stop flicking dirt!" Deanna yelled at her brother Jonathan.

"Sorry," Jonathan said, drawing pictures in the soil with a stick.

"How can you stand playing in dirt all the time?" Deanna asked.

"Dirt's the best!" Jonathan exclaimed.

"Maybe five-year-olds like it," Deanna said. "Right, Michelle?"

Deanna's 13-year-old sister sat on the front porch, putting another coat of pink nail polish on her toes.

"Huh? Yeah. Five," Michelle mumbled.

Her mind was always somewhere else.

Jonathan poured water on the dirt to make mud. He laughed as he jumped in and squished the mud between his toes.

Deanna's father was always saying that soil was valuable. Her family made their living growing vegetables. Every spring Dad would crumble the soil. "There's a lot of life in there," Dad would say.

Deanna was sick of dirt. It just reminded her of chores to do on the farm.

"Enough about dirt," groaned Deanna.

"What about dirt?" a tiny voice squeaked.

"Who said that?" Deanna asked. Michelle's nose was buried in a magazine so she hadn't said it. Deanna knew it wasn't Jonathan's voice either.

"I said it," the tiny voice repeated. Deanna looked around.

"Down here."

Deanna looked down and saw an ant standing in front of her.

She looked closer.

"That's right. It was me," the ant said. Deanna couldn't believe that the ant was speaking!

"Are you talking to me?" Deanna asked.

"Yes," the ant answered. "I heard you complain. You're rather silly. You don't know how interesting dirt is!"

"Dirt? Interesting? Hah!" Deanna snorted.

"Would you like to see how interesting?" the ant asked.

"Actually I would," Deanna replied.

"Shall we invite the other two?" the ant asked.

"Jonathan," Deanna called. "This talking ant here wants to know if we'd like to go underground with him."

The ant nodded his head and said, "Hello, young fellow."

Jonathan dropped a pebble he was tossing. "OK! Let's go," he said.

"How about you, Michelle?"

"Huh? Ant," Michelle mumbled as she read her magazine.

Deanna rolled her eyes and said, "Never mind her."

"Now close your eyes," the ant instructed. "Repeat after me: *Make me as small as an ant.*"

Suddenly Deanna and Jonathan were next to Jonathan's pebble. It looked like a boulder.

"Follow me," the ant said, waving one of his six legs.

Deanna and Jonathan followed him deep into a cavern. They entered a huge chamber where a large ant was lying down while smaller ants bustled around her.

"Shh. This is our Queen," the ant whispered. "And these are the workers who care for her."

They crept through a tunnel to a chamber with a
lot of wiggly, wormy creatures.

"This is our nursery," the ant said. "The baby ants
are taken care of here."

They followed the tunnel deeper into the cavern.

"This is where we stay during winter," the ant said.

"I wish I could do that," Deanna said.

"Well, what do you think?" the ant asked.

"It's like a subterranean city," Deanna replied.

"Now, I'll take you back," said the ant.

They climbed to the surface. "Close your eyes. Repeat after me: *I'm no longer small like an ant.*"

Instantly, Deanna and Jonathan were their normal sizes.

"Farewell!" the ant said, as he returned to his subterranean home.

"What's going on?" Michelle asked.

"Well, it has to do with dirt," Jonathan said.

"Bor-ing," said Michelle, rolling her eyes.

"Maybe. But Dad's right. There's a lot of life in this dirt," Deanna said.

What Do You Think?

What do Deanna and Jonathan see underground?

CAVE'S END

Bill Stone explores deep caves. He leads teams that explore cave tunnels and chambers for weeks and weeks.

Stone's team trains for months before a long cave adventure. They walk, run, bike, and climb stairs to make sure their bodies are ready to survive in a deep cave.

Bill Stone makes sure the team carries plenty of supplies. The group brings food that does not need to be cooked.

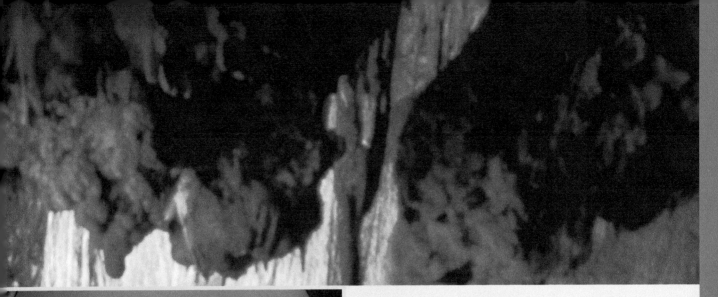

It takes yards of rope to go up and down cave walls. The team also needs to be able to see. No sunlight gets in where they hike. They bring a good supply of rope, batteries, and flashlights.

A machine called the Rebreather helps cavers breathe in places where there isn't much oxygen. The Rebreather tank can last longer than most diving tanks.

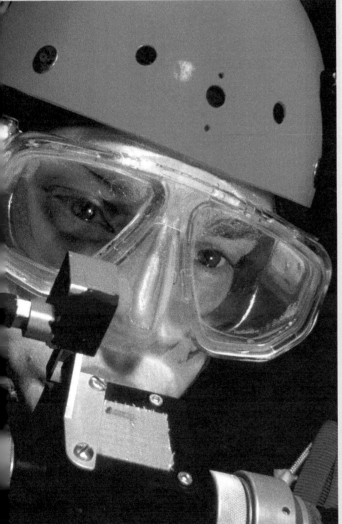

This Rebreather allows cave explorers to search for longer periods of time.

When cave explorers enter a cave, they map where passageways, chambers, and stalactites and stalagmites are. These maps help other explorers.

Stone led a group of explorers through Cheve (CHAY-vay) Cave in Mexico. Some think it's the deepest cave in the world. Bill Stone's team proved that Cheve Cave is the deepest in the Americas.

Cave explorers make maps of caves to help other explorers.

What are people who explore caves called?

spelunker goes in caves, but is not trained

speleologist* explores caves as a job; collects data

Is Bill Stone a spelunker or a speleologist?

***speleologist** spee-lee-OL-uh-jist

Crystal Cave
and Bear Den, Canyon Wide and Dusty Breakdown caves
Plan View, Showing passages as polygons colored to illustrate relative elevations

Passage elevations are based upon survey elevations. Divisions between layers (colors) were chosen based upon levels within the cave. Level elevations are relative to station A1, zero datum.

Upper levels are shown in preference to lower levels. Bedrock pillars and "islands" on upper levels are shown as transparent and thus often reveal lower level passages.

Surveyed June, July, August, and September 1995, July and August 1996 and August 1997. See the sheet "Line Plot and Survey History" for information on survey dates and personnel.

Data processed by Compass software, produced by Larry Fish. Drafted on Coreldraw 7 by Joel Despain. December 1996, March 1997 and March 1998.

White (highest level) 50 to 61.9 meters.
Sand; 40 to 50 meters
Yellow; 28 to 40 meters
Olive; 18 to 28 meters
Light Green; 13 to 18 meters
Green; 5 to 13 meters
Black (lowest level) -4.6 to 5 meters

4 you 2 Do

Word Play

Use the letters in the words below to make a list of supplies that underground explorers need. Here's one: lights

underground
cavern
chamber
stalactite

Making Connections

How is Deanna's exploration like exploring caves? How is it different?

On Paper

Pretend you are a famous cave explorer on an exploration. Describe what you would see.

Possible Answers to Word Play: helmets, cameras, rebreather.

GO FOR THE GOLD!

GOLD · 1987

GOLD · 1988

Contents

GO FOR THE GOLD!

Let's Explore

Words 2 the Wise

The **California Gold Rush** changed the way people thought about gold. As you read, think about how gold affects peoples' lives today.

Let's Explore

GOLD

The Search for Gold

People started searching for golden nuggets at least as far back as 3100 B.C. The fascination with gold caught on quickly. The first known treasure map was found in Egypt. It had pictures of a gold mine in a mountain.

Today many companies mine for gold in Asia and Australia.

Gold Accessories

People have used gold for centuries to make jewelry and crowns. When people thought of gold, they thought of wealth. People wanted anything made of the shiny metal. They made plates, cups, vases, and other objects out of gold.

Kings and queens wore gold as a sign of their wealth and power.

Money

The first gold coin was made around 700 B.C. These coins were exchanged for goods. Coins made trading much easier. They were easy to carry.

Gold coins are still produced today. Many people collect them.

Many pounds of gold were used to build the USS *Columbia* space shuttle.

Gold and Technology

Today gold has many other uses. Gold is used to make computers, DVDs, cameras, and mobile phones. Gold is also used on satellites and on jet engines.

Air Force One, the airplane used by the President of the United States, is protected from missiles by gold-plated reflectors. Most cockpit windows are coated with a thin film of gold to protect pilots from the sun's rays and extreme temperatures.

People can eat gold flakes, but doctors say not to eat a lot of them.

Golden Meals

Flakes of gold are added to some desserts and drinks. That makes them very expensive, but some people think they are worth the price.

Golden Awards

Gold medals are given to the first place winners in the Olympics. And the World Cup of Soccer trophy is made of solid gold.

The highest award Olympic athletes can win is a gold medal.

TO CALIFORNIA!

BY JULIE LAVENDER

It was 1848. Headlines told everyone the news. Someone had discovered gold in California!

Suddenly, everyone was thinking about moving West. People called it "gold fever." Within a year thousands of people had left their homes and jobs. The Gold Rush of 1849 had begun.

How could people get to California? No railroad crossed from east to west yet. These gold-seekers tried every route they could think of. Nothing could stop them!

OREGON-CALIFORNIA TRAIL

The Oregon-California Trail stretched from Missouri to the West.

A ROUTE OVER LAND

Many gold-seekers took a route called the Oregon-California Trail. A few men went alone on horseback. But most traveled as groups in covered wagons that were pulled by oxen or mules. They faced much hardship. It took six or seven months to get to California this way.

Gold-seekers left jobs in towns, cities, and on farms. The dream of gold made them take risks. They faced bad storms, rough terrain, and scorching heat.

Travelers packed supplies in wagons and headed west to look for gold.

They rode on muddy, bumpy roads. They crossed mountains, deserts, and rivers. It was a difficult and dangerous route.

The trip was hard on the animals as well as the people. The travelers loaded the wagons with extra clothes and dishes. Back home these things were necessities, but on the trail the lives of the animals were more important. The travelers threw heavy things away to lighten the load.

The Oregon-California Trail crossed rivers and mountains.

A ROUTE OVER THE SEA

Many gold-seekers took a water route that began in New York. The ships sailed down the coast of North America and around South America. The journey was about 15,000 miles and took four to eight months.

At first the boat trips seemed like an easier way to travel west. There was food on board, and people entertained the gold-seekers with speeches. However, the ships sometimes ran out of food and water. Passengers ate spoiled or wormy food.

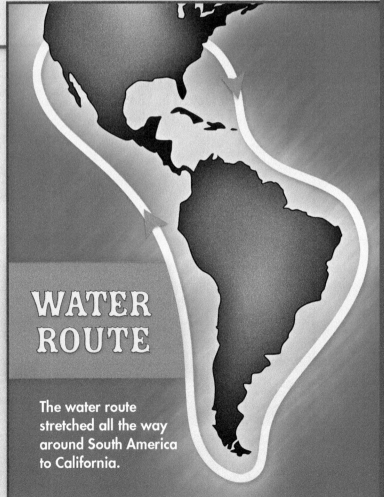

WATER ROUTE

The water route stretched all the way around South America to California.

Passengers were not used to long sea voyages. They got seasick from the ship's motion. They became infected with diseases and got sick from diets without fruits or vegetables. Some died on board. Their bodies were wrapped in cloth and buried at sea.

The ships finally reached California. The passengers were still far from the gold fields. They would walk the last part of the long journey. The gold fever kept them going!

This is how San Francisco harbor looked in 1849, when the Gold Rush started.

A ROUTE BETWEEN TWO CONTINENTS

A third route was by both sea and land! It was called the Panama shortcut. To take the shortcut, ships headed south along the Atlantic coast. They did not go all the way around South America. Ships stopped in Panama, a narrow strip of land between North and South America. Then travelers had to walk through jungles to get to the Pacific Ocean.

Another ship waited on the other side.

PANAMA SHORTCUT

CALIFORNIA

NEW YORK CITY

The Panama shortcut started on the Atlantic coast and took the gold seekers west to the Pacific Ocean.

PANAMA

Travelers paid people who lived in Panama to guide them across a river in canoes. After travelers crossed the river, they trudged through the hot, wet jungle.

At first they were excited to see strange jungle plants and animals. But this route was filled with hardship. Many died from sickness before they reached the gold fields. The route was shorter, but it was still very difficult.

Each of the three routes was difficult in its own way. Of the thousands that set out to find gold, many never reached California. Some who did reach California found gold. Others did not. But they were all part of a famous time in the history of the United States—the California Gold Rush of 1849.

WHAT DO YOU THINK?

What made the routes to California so difficult?

STRIKING It RICH

by John Conger

The California Gold Rush brought many people West in search of gold. But gold wasn't the only way to strike it rich!

Samuel Brannan bought every shovel in a small town near where gold was found. Then he ran through the streets yelling "Gold! Gold!"

People rushed to buy shovels! Then they would claim a spot of land as their own and start digging. Brannan made a lot of money selling shovels!

The Forty-Niners

The gold-seekers were called "the forty-niners" because they left home in 1849.

Boarding houses offered a place to stay to gold-seekers.

Word about gold spread throughout the United States and the world. People left their homes and rushed to claim land in California.

When the first gold-seekers arrived, they needed somewhere to live. Many newcomers stayed at boarding houses. They rented rooms and got meals. The boarders, or renters, ate together. They shared news. Who had struck it rich? Who had given up and returned home? The owners of the boarding houses earned more money than ever before.

Towns grew as people moved to California looking for gold.

Before the news that there was gold in California, only a few hundred people lived in the area. After the news, 30 homes might be built in a day!

The building of homes caused other businesses to start. Carpenters were needed to build houses. They needed materials to build them. Hardware stores opened to sell supplies.

Other enterprises developed. One woman bought a stove and boards for tables, and she cooked meals for hungry miners. She earned money fast!

Ghirardelli

Ghirardelli Square, named for Domingo Ghirardelli, is a national historic landmark.

Grocery stores opened so the miners could pack up food for days. But the prices were very high. One egg was almost fifty cents. You can buy about four eggs for fifty cents today.

One miner who dug for gold was Domingo Ghirardelli (doe-MIN-go JEER-uh-del-lee). When he had no luck finding it, he remembered the chocolates he used to make with his father in Italy. He opened a chocolate company in San Francisco. His famous chocolates are still sold today!

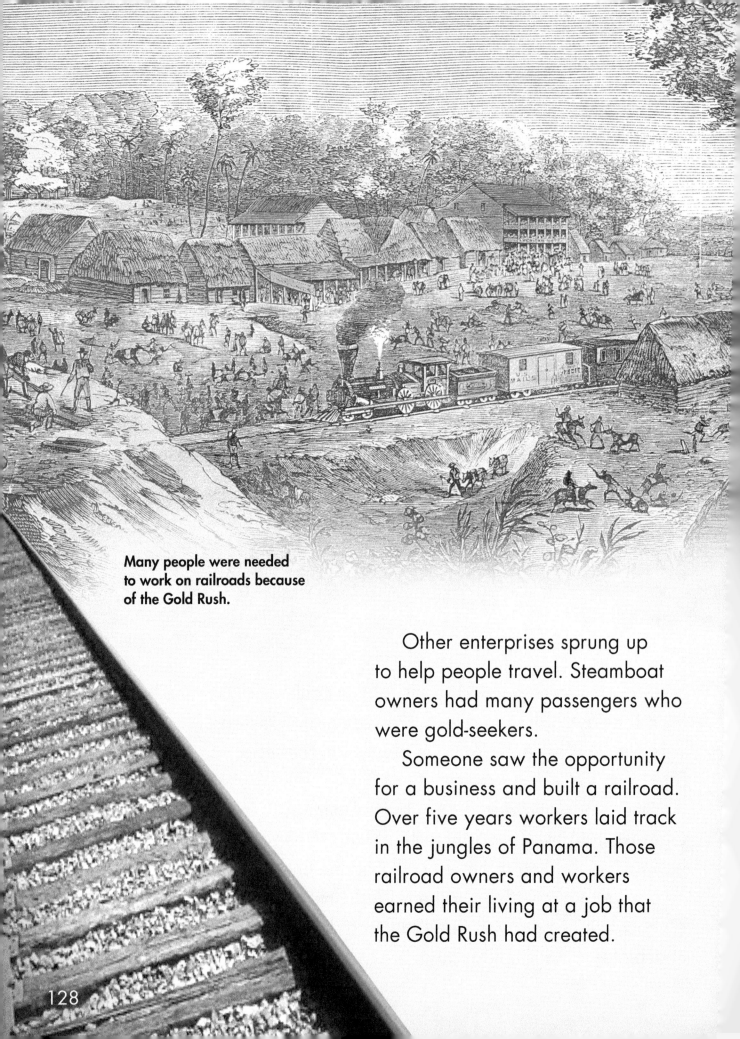

Many people were needed
to work on railroads because
of the Gold Rush.

Other enterprises sprung up
to help people travel. Steamboat
owners had many passengers who
were gold-seekers.

Someone saw the opportunity
for a business and built a railroad.
Over five years workers laid track
in the jungles of Panama. Those
railroad owners and workers
earned their living at a job that
the Gold Rush had created.

Miners would go to the bank to have their gold weighed.

The Gold Rush brought many jobs. People had money to spend. Soon they didn't have to worry about a place to stay and food to eat.

But they needed a place to keep the money. Banks are a necessity in any town. Henry Wells and William Fargo started their enterprise, the Wells Fargo Bank. It was another business that started during the Gold Rush and still exists today!

Metal rivets on pants were something new. Levi Strauss thought this was a great idea.

Levi Strauss moved to San Francisco to start a new business. He sold dry goods to stores that were popping up all over the West. Jacob Davis was one of his customers. He bought cloth to make work pants.

Jacob used metal rivets to make the pants stronger. Miners really liked these pants! Jacob asked Levi to be his business partner. Their partnership led to the birth of blue jeans.

The stores and restaurants of mining towns were busy during the Gold Rush.

News of the California Gold Rush spread and changed the United States forever. It changed people's lives too. Many dreamed of becoming rich overnight in California. For some gold-seekers, their dreams came true in ways that they had never expected!

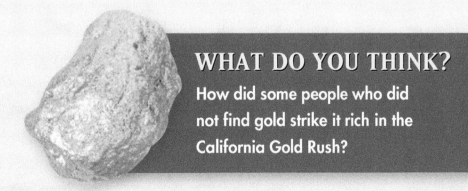

WHAT DO YOU THINK?

How did some people who did not find gold strike it rich in the California Gold Rush?

The Hard, Gold Facts

Here are some interesting facts about gold.

If you win a gold medal in the Olympics, it is not solid gold. The last year that Olympic medals were made of solid gold was 1912.

If an ounce of gold were stretched into a wire, it would be 3 miles long! That's 12 times around a track.

LAPS 12

Fort Knox in Kentucky is where the United States government stores most of its gold. Fort Knox has around 147 million ounces of gold bars and coins. That's worth more than 6 trillion dollars!

If you collected all the gold ever mined in the history of the world and put it in one place, it would be a cube weighing 190 million pounds. It would cover an area of 19 square yards!

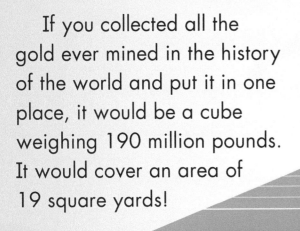

Where's the best place to find gold? Maybe it's underwater! Scientists think that the oceans hold as much as 70 million tons of gold! The problem is, how do you get to it?

The heaviest piece of gold ever found weighed over 156 pounds! That's as heavy as a person.

4 You 2 Do

Word Play

Pick a word or phrase that begins with each letter in the word *claim* to describe the Gold Rush.

California
L
A
I
M

Making Connections

Compare the dreams of gold-seekers with the dreams of those who opened new stores and businesses.

On Paper

If you lived in 1849, would you have gone West to seek gold? Explain why or why not.

Possible answers to Word Play: land, long trip; animals, across water; illness, injury, in jungles; money

Glossary

as·ton·ish (ə ston′ ish), *VERB.* to surprise greatly; amaze: *We were astonished at the force of the wind during the hurricane.* **as·ton·ished, as·ton·ish·ing.**

as·tro·naut (as′ trə nòt), *NOUN.* a member of the crew of a spacecraft: *While in space, astronauts repair space stations and do experiments.* *PL.* **as·tro·nauts.**

cav·ern (kav′ ərn), *NOUN.* a large cave: *We had to use flashlights to see in the cavern.*

cen·tur·y (sen′ chər ē), *NOUN.* a period of 100 years: *The twentieth century was from 1901 to 2000.* *PL.* **cen·tur·ies.**

a in hat	ō in open	sh in she
ā in age	ȯ in all	th in thin
â in care	ô in order	ŦH in then
ä in far	oi in oil	zh in measure
e in let	ou in out	ə =a in about
ē in equal	u in cup	ə =e in taken
ėr in term	u̇ in put	ə =i in pencil
i in it	ü in rule	ə =o in lemon
ī in ice	ch in child	ə =u in circus
o in hot	ng in long	

cham·ber (chām′ bər), *NOUN.* a large underground cavern; a room: *The explorers entered each chamber of the cave.*

claim (klām), *VERB.* to demand as your own or your right: *The settlers claimed the land beyond the river as theirs.*

com·pan·ion (kəm pan′ yən), *NOUN.* someone who goes along with or spends time with you; someone who shares in what you are doing: *The twins were companions in work and play.* PL. **com·pan·ions.**

con·sum·er (kən sü′ mər), *NOUN.* someone who buys and uses food, clothing, or anything grown or made by someone else: *Children are consumers when they buy their favorite toys.* PL. **con·sum·ers.**

crew (krü), *NOUN.* a group of people who work together: *The space shuttle's crew completed several experiments.*

drill (dril), *NOUN.* a way of teaching or training by having people practice something over and over: *The school had several fire drills to make sure everyone knew what to do.*

en·ter·prise (en′ tər prīz), *NOUN.* any undertaking; a project; a business: *Other enterprises, such as boarding houses and hardware stores, sprang up during the California Gold Rush.*

e·quip·ment (i kwip′ mənt), *NOUN.* what someone or something is supplied with; supplies: *We keep our camping equipment in order.*

a in hat	ō in open	sh in she
ā in age	ȯ in all	th in thin
â in care	ô in order	ᴛʜ in then
ä in far	oi in oil	zh in measure
e in let	ou in out	ə =a in about
ē in equal	u in cup	ə =e in taken
ėr in term	u̇ in put	ə =i in pencil
i in it	ü in rule	ə =o in lemon
ī in ice	ch in child	ə =u in circus
o in hot	ng in long	

ex·pe·di·tion (ek′ spə dish′ ən), NOUN. a long, well-planned trip for a special purpose: *The astronauts spent several months getting ready for the expedition to Mars.*

ex·plo·ra·tion (ek′ splə rā′ shən), NOUN. a way of traveling in unknown lands, seas, or in outer space in order to discover new things: *Astronauts take part in space exploration.*

grot·to (grot′ ō), NOUN. cave or cavern. PL. **grot·toes or grot·tos.**

hard·ship (härd′ ship), NOUN. something hard to bear; hard condition of living: *Hunger, cold, and sickness were the hardships pioneers faced.*

138

his·to·ri·cal (hi stôr′ ə kəl),
ADJECTIVE.

1 based on history: *He likes to read historical novels about the Gold Rush.*
2 known to be real or true; in history, not in legend: *Is the story of King Arthur myth or historical fact?*

jour·ney (jėr′ nē), NOUN. a long trip from one place to another: *The journey from New York to California took several days.* PL. **jour·neys.**

lo·cate (lō′ kāt), VERB. to find out exactly where something is: *The rescue team used a cell phone signal to locate the lost hiker.*

ne·ces·si·ty (nə ses′ ə tē), NOUN. something that is needed: *Water is a necessity of life.*

a in hat	ō in open	sh in she
ā in age	ȯ in all	th in thin
â in care	ô in order	ŦH in then
ä in far	oi in oil	zh in measure
e in let	ou in out	ə =a in about
ē in equal	u in cup	ə =e in taken
ėr in term	u̇ in put	ə =i in pencil
i in it	ü in rule	ə =o in lemon
ī in ice	ch in child	ə =u in circus
o in hot	ng in long	

or·bit (ôr′ bit), VERB. to travel around the Earth or some other astronomical object: *Some artificial satellites can orbit the Earth in less than an hour.* **or·bit·ed, or·bit·ing.**

prod·uct (prod′ əkt), NOUN. something that someone makes or grows: *Grain is a farm product.* PL. **prod·ucts.**

pro·gram (prō′ gram), NOUN. a plan for what is going to be done: *The U.S. space program is planning a trip to Mars.*

re-cre·ate (rē′ krē āt′), VERB. to make a thing that has already been made: *The students will re-create the first Thanksgiving for their class play.* **re-cre·at·ed, re-cre·at·ing.**

re·en·act·ment (rē′ en akt′ mənt), NOUN. a performance in which people act out a past event: *We watched a reenactment of the Battle of Gettysburg.*

ren·dez·vous (rän′ də vü), *NOUN*. a meeting planned at a certain time and place: *A rendezvous in orbit was planned for the two spacecraft.*

route (rüt, rout), *NOUN*. a way that you choose to get somewhere: *Which route do you take to get home from school?*

shut·tle (shut′ l), *NOUN*. a bus, train, or airplane that runs back and forth over a short distance; **space shuttle,** a spacecraft with wings, which can orbit the Earth, land like an airplane, and can be used again: *The shuttle carried the astronauts to the moon.*

a in hat	ō in open	sh in she
ā in age	o̊ in all	th in thin
â in care	ô in order	ŦH in then
ä in far	oi in oil	zh in measure
e in let	ou in out	ə =a in about
ē in equal	u in cup	ə =e in taken
ėr in term	u̇ in put	ə =i in pencil
i in it	ü in rule	ə =o in lemon
ī in ice	ch in child	ə =u in circus
o in hot	ng in long	

sta·lac·tite (stə lak′ tīt), *NOUN.*
a formation of stone, shaped like
an icicle, hanging from the roof
of a cave. It is formed by minerals
in dripping water.

sta·lag·mite (stə lag′ mīt), *NOUN.*
a formation of stone, shaped like
a cone, built up on the floor of a
cave. It is formed by minerals in
dripping water.

sub·ter·ra·ne·an (sub′ tə rā′ nē ən), *ADJECTIVE.* underground:
A subterranean passage led from the castle to a cave.

track (trak), *VERB.* to follow something by means of footprints,
smell, or any mark left by anything that has passed by:
The dog enjoyed tracking the rabbit through the garden.
tracked, track·ing.

tra·di·tion (trə dish′ ən), *NOUN.* a custom or belief that is
learned from grandparents and parents: *Making cupcakes
is a birthday tradition in my family.*

trail (trāl), NOUN. a path across a field or through the woods: *The scouts followed the trail for days.*

tun·nel (tun′ l), NOUN. an underground passage: *Traffic passes through a tunnel under the river.*

un·der·ground (un′ dər ground′), ADVERB. beneath the surface of the ground: *Most miners work underground.*

a in hat	ō in open	sh in she
ā in age	ȯ in all	th in thin
â in care	ô in order	ŦH in then
ä in far	oi in oil	zh in measure
e in let	ou in out	ə =a in about
ē in equal	u in cup	ə =e in taken
ėr in term	u̇ in put	ə =i in pencil
i in it	ü in rule	ə =o in lemon
ī in ice	ch in child	ə =u in circus
o in hot	ng in long	

Acknowledgments

Text

Every effort has been made to locate the copyright owner of material reproduced in this component. Omissions brought to our attention will be corrected in subsequent editions. Grateful acknowledgment is made to the following for copyrighted material.

80 Dutton Children's Books, A division of Penguin Group (USA), Inc. "How Strange It Is" from *Poems of Earth and Space* by Claudia Lewis. Copyright © 1967 by Claudia Lewis. Used by permission of Dutton Children's Books, a Division of Penguin Young Readers Group, a Member of Penguin Group (USA) Inc., 345 Hudson Street, New York, NY 10014. All rights reserved.

81 Houghton Mifflin Harcourt "Night Sky" by Zaro Weil from *Mud, Moon and Me*. Text copyright © 1989 by Zaro Weil. Used by permission of Houghton Mifflin Harcourt Publishing Company. All rights reserved.

Illustrations

6, 18–25 Maurie Manning; **29** Susan J. Carlson; **44–50** Ruth Palmer; **74, 132, 133** Rob Schuster; **84, 96–103** Lynda Cohen.

Photographs

Every effort has been made to secure permission and provide appropriate credit for photographic material. The publisher deeply regrets any omission and pledges to correct errors called to its attention in subsequent editions.

Unless otherwise acknowledged, all photographs are the property of Pearson Education, Inc.

Photo locators denoted as follows: Top (T), Center (C), Bottom (B), Left (L), Right (R), Background (Bkgd)

Cover (B) ©Getty's Digitized NASA Images/Getty Images, (TL) Corbis, (TR) George H.H. Huey/Corbis, (CR) Stephen Frink/Index Stock Imagery, (CL) Stockbyte Platinum/Getty Images; **1** (CL) Getty Images; **2** (CR) Hemera Technologies, (BR) Ron Chapple/Getty Images; **3** (B) ©Bryce Flynn Photography Inc/Getty Images, (TL) ©Getty's Digitized NASA Images/Getty Images, (CR) Stephen Alvarez/Getty Images; **5** (Bkgd) George H.H. Huey/Corbis, (CL) Getty Images; **6** (TR) Corbis, (BR) Getty Images, (TCR) Hemera Technologies, (BR) Hemera Technologies/Thinkstock; **8** (T) Jason Reed/Reuters/Corbis; **9** (TR, CR, BR) Brooks Kraft/Corbis, (BL) Corbis; **10** (BR, B) ©Courtesy Great River Road, (TL, CR) Hemera Technologies; **11** (T) ©Charles Cook Photography; **12** (BC) ©Charles Cook Photography, (TL) Hemera Technologies; **13** (TR) Hemera Technologies, (C) Paul A. Souders/Corbis; **14** (TL) ©Andre Jenny/Alamy Images, (TR) ©Courtesy Great River Road, (B) Hemera Technologies; **15** (TR) Hemera Technologies, (B) Richard I'Anson/Getty Images; **16** (B) ©Courtesy Great River Road, (TL) Hemera Technologies; **17** (CR) ©Richard T. Nowitz/Corbis, (C) Bob Krist/Corbis, (TR) Hemera Technologies; **26** (Bkgd) ©Gunter Marx Photography/Corbis, (CL) Getty Images, (TR) Hemera Technologies/Thinkstock; **27** (TL) Getty Images; **28** (Bkgd) ©Gunter Marx Photography/Corbis, (T) ©Smithsonian American Art Museum, Washington, DC/Art Resource, NY, (CR) Getty Images; **29** (TL) Getty Images; **30** (BR) Rudi Von Briel/PhotoEdit; **31** (Bkgd) David Parker/Photo Researchers, Inc.; **32** (CR) Bettmann/Corbis, (TR) Corbis, (BC) Hemera Technologies; **33** (L) Stephen Frink/Index Stock Imagery; **34** (CR) ©Royalty-Free/Corbis, (BR) AP/Wide World Photos, (C) Corbis, (CL) Getty Images; **35** (BR) David R. Frazier Photolibrary, Inc./Alamy Images, (B) Ron Chapple/Getty Images, (CR) Thomas Hartwell/SABA/Corbis; **36** (L) Bettmann/Corbis; **37** (Bkgd) Stephen Frink/Index Stock Imagery; **38** (Bkgd) Alexis Rosenfeld/Photo Researchers, Inc.; **39** (T) Getty Images; **40** (Bkgd) Philip de Bay/Historical Picture Archive/Corbis; **41** (TR) Detlev Van Ravensway/Photo Researchers, Inc., (T) Getty Images; **42** (Bkgd) ©Mikenorton/Shutterstock; **43** (B) Andrew Fox/Corbis, (T) Getty Images; **52** (BC) Sinibomb Images/Alamy Images, (BR) Spencer Platt/Getty Images; **53** (T) Lionel Derimais/Sygma/Corbis; **54** (CR) Hemera Technologies, (B) Peter Menzel/Photo Researchers, Inc.; **55** (T) Andreas Rentz/Getty Images; **56** (BR) Stephen Frink/

Index Stock Imagery; **57** (Bkgd) Getty Images; **58** (TR) age fotostock/SuperStock, (C, BCR) Hemera Technologies, (CR) NASA/Photo Researchers, Inc.; **59** NASA; **60** (Bkgd) eStock Photo/Alamy Images; **61** (C) eStock Photo/Alamy Images; **62** (Bkgd) age fotostock/SuperStock; **63** (T) NASA Johnson Space Center/NASA Image Exchange; **64** (CL) ©Getty's Digitized NASA Images/Getty Images, (Bkgd) Getty Images; **65** (T) NASA, (CR) NASA/Photo Researchers, Inc.; **66** (TR) Hemera Technologies, (C) NASA; **67** (TR) NASA; **68** (TL) Larry Keenan Associates/Getty Images, (TL) NASA; **69** (B) Larry Keenan Associates/Getty Images; **70** (Bkgd) Art Montes De Oca/Getty Images, (B) Joe Drivas/Getty Images, (TC) NASA; **71** (BC) ©Getty's Digitized NASA Images/Getty Images, (TR) NASA; **72** (TL, Bkgd) Getty Images, (BC) Hemera Technologies; **73** (B) D2 Productions/Getty Images, (CR, BR) Hemera Technologies; **74** (BR) Don Mason/Corbis, (Bkgd) Getty Images; **75** (BC) Paul Viant/Getty Images; **76** (Bkgd) Getty Images, (BC) IT Stock; **77** (BL) Hemera Technologies, (BR) Jupiter Images; **78** (Bkgd) Getty Images, (BL) JLP/Sylvia Torres/Corbis; **79** (C) Digital image ©1996 CORBIS; Original image courtesy of NASA/Corbis, (CR) Hemera Technologies; **80** (T) Getty Images; **81** (TR) Getty Images; **82** NASA; **83** (Bkgd) ©Gabriel M. Covian/The Image Bank/Getty Images; **84** (TR) ©Royalty-Free/Corbis, (BR) Hemera Technologies, (CR) Robert Harding Picture Library Ltd/Alamy Images; **85** (L) Gerald Favre/Gerald Favre; **86** (Bkgd) ©Royalty-Free/Corbis, (BL) Getty Images, (CR) Glyn Thomas/Alamy Images; **87** (CR) ©Royalty-Free/Corbis, (B) Jeremy Hoare/Alamy Images; **88** (Bkgd) Bill Hatcher/National Geographic Image Collection, (R) Getty Images; **89** (BR) Frans Lanting Photography, (CR) Luis Veiga/Getty Images, (T) Oliver Strewe/Lonely Planet Images; **90** (Bkgd) Getty Images, (T) Robert Harding Picture Library Ltd/Alamy Images; **91** (T) ©dfwalls/Alamy; **92** (T) Buffalo Bill Historical Center, Cody, Wyoming / 70.86/The Art Archive, (Bkgd) Getty Images; **93** (T) Stuart Redler/Getty Images, (CL) Underwood & Underwood/Corbis; **94** (Bkgd) Getty Images, (T) Hulton-Deutsch Collection/Corbis; **95** (T) Stephen Alvarez/National Geographic Image Collection; **104** (Bkgd) ©Demetrio Carrasco/Getty Images; **105** (CL) Chris A Crumley/Alamy Images, (BR) Hemera Technologies; **106** (CL) Chad Ehlers/Getty Images, (Bkgd) Gavin Hellier/Getty Images, (BL) Stephen Alvarez/Getty Images; **107** (TL) Hemera Technologies, (L) Michele Westmorland/Getty Images, (BR) National Park Service; **108** (BR) Gerald Favre/Gerald Favre ; **109** (Bkgd) Peter M. Fisher/Corbis; **110** (TR) ©Royalty-Free/Corbis, (C) Getty Images, (BR) Hemera Technologies, (CR) North Wind Picture Archives; **111** (B) Dave G. Houser/Post-Houserstock/Corbis, (TR) Matthew Polak/Corbis; **112** (B) ©Bryce Flynn Photography Inc/Getty Images, (CR) Colin Keates/Courtesy of the Natural History Museum, London/©DK Images, (Bkgd) Hemera Technologies; **113** (CR) ©Royalty-Free/Corbis, (BR) Dave King/©DK Images; **114** (T, BR) Hemera Technologies, (T) NASA Kennedy Space Center/NASA Image Exchange; **115** (TR) AP/Wide World Photos, (B) Ben Fink/Foodpix/Jupiter Images; **116** (T) Getty Images; **117** (Bkgd) ©Hulton Archive/Getty Images; **118** (Bkgd) Corbis, (T) Getty Images; **120** (Bkgd) Corbis; **121** (TR) Getty Images; **122** (Bkgd) ©Bettmann/Corbis, (T) Getty Images, (C) North Wind Picture Archives; **123** (BR) Getty Images; **124** (Bkgd) Getty Images, (B) Mary Evans Picture Library/Alamy Images; **125** (T) Mike Kipling Photography/Alamy Images; **126** (T) Corbis, (TL) DK Images, (TC) Hemera Technologies; **127** (T) ©Steve Hamblin/Alamy, (CR, C) Getty Images, (TR) Hemera Technologies; **128** (BL) Hemera Technologies, (T) The Granger Collection, NY; **129** (CR) Hemera Technologies, (T) North Wind Picture Archives; **130** (TL) SuperStock; **131** (T) Brown Brothers, (C) Getty Images; **134** (BR) Dave G. Houser/Post-Houserstock/Corbis; **135** (CR) NASA Marshall Space Flight Center/NASA Image Exchange; **136** (BR) NASA, (TR) Stephen Alvarez/National Geographic Image Collection; **138** (BR) ©Courtesy Great River Road, (CR) Getty Images; **139** (TR) Brown Brothers; **140** (TR) Detlev Van Ravensway/Photo Researchers, Inc., (BR) Richard I'Anson/Getty Images; **141** (CR) ©Getty's Digitized NASA Images/Getty Images; **142** (CR) Frans Lanting Photography, (TR) Oliver Strewe/Lonely Planet Images; **143** (C) ©Gabriel M. Covian/The Image Bank/Getty Images, (TR) Ron Chapple/Getty Images.